MW01166047

Beyond Competence

The Character of an Off-Roading Coach

Compiled by Scott Frickenstein,
PhD, PCC

DEDICATION

This book is dedicated to
Cheryl Scanlan—
our beloved mentor, coach, and leader—
whose example we follow,
as she follows the example of Christ.
(1 Corinthians 11:1)

TABLE OF CONTENTS

FOREWORD

Ten years ago, I was wrapping up an all-day training in Southern California on leadership coaching with my dear friend and colleague Cheryl Scanlan, and we were fielding final questions from the executive coaches in attendance. The training had been a smashing success, and several were enthusiastically offering their praise. As the last one wrapped up his comments, I glanced over my shoulder to smile at Cheryl, only to find that she had left the room. True to form, she had given her all—her knowledge and expertise along with her heart and soul—and she had made a hasty departure in lieu of collapsing.

Cheryl and I had first met years before, following a talk I gave in which I referenced my battle with advanced Lyme disease. As a fellow sufferer, she had prayed that the Lord would make it clear if she was to connect with me, and the Holy Spirit wasted no time in arranging for us to be the only two people in the large cafeteria at the conference center. Our mutual health struggles were soon eclipsed by our mutual passion for coaching and our love of the Lord, and we became fast friends.

Since I knew Cheryl's departure following our talk was surely due to Lyme exhaustion, I simply touched base by phone to check on her, and we made plans to reconnect the following morning over breakfast. My wife and I retired early to bed but were soon awakened by an ambulance at the resort and then a phone call from Cheryl's husband, Tom, back in North Carolina. He explained that Cheryl was being rushed to an area hospital and had a travel folder with her that contained medical instructions for just such an emergency; he wondered if we might take a cab there to serve as her advocates in his absence, and we naturally agreed. The crisis resolved as so many of our health scares have, and we notched yet one more adventure together in advancing the field of coaching through the very imperfect "vessels of clay" that we are.

I share that story because it illustrates a basic premise of the book you hold in your hand—that our "doing" can never really be separated from our "being." Our doing *flows from* and *testifies to* our being. "Show me your faith without your works, and I will show you my faith by my works" (James 2:18, NKJV). Each of us can fake it for a while, but our actions ultimately reveal our true nature, our essence, and our character.

Cheryl and I had taught that day on professional-grade, distinctly Christian coaching—but our conveyance of the skills, tools, and techniques would not have resonated so strongly if we had not authentically shared our "selves." Part of the training was taught; a great deal more of it was caught. Cheryl had "left it all on the field" that day as her being and her doing were united in powerful teaching and coaching.

This book is a collection of shared stories and interviews from professional Christian coaches on the *ontological* side of coaching. Ontology is the metaphysical study of "being" (personhood) and of "becoming." Many excellent coaching books have been written over the past 25 years, but the vast majority have focused principally on the "what" and the "how"—the "doing"; what we must *do* in order to coach well. Very few have addressed who we must *be* and *become* in order to coach well.

Our motto at Professional Christian Coaching Institute (PCCI) is "Raising the Standard," and this collection of character qualities necessary for masterful Christian coaching is a needed work toward that end. As originally envisioned by author/compiler Scott Frickenstein, however, this book is also a public attestation to the work and influence of Cheryl, a pioneer in our field and an International Coaching Federation (ICF) Master Certified Coach (MCC). As Christian coaches, we are called to excel in both our competence and our character. In this volume, you'll see what it looks like when competent coaches who exhibit Christlike character partner with the Holy Spirit in serving others.

Scott and his fellow contributors took a collaborative "coach approach" in writing this book, exploring the content together through interviews and discussions, sharpening each other's chapters via peer editing, and celebrating what happened in their own coaching when they took real-time steps to grow in these qualities. As I read the manuscript, I was encouraged and "spurred on" to continue my own journey of becoming more Christlike in my coaching. I hope you will be similarly challenged as you enjoy this book written by coaches, for coaches!

—Chris McCluskey, PCC, President
Professional Christian Coaching Institute
April 2023, Edgar Springs, Missouri

INTRODUCTION

"...respect those who labor among you and are over you in the Lord and admonish you, and esteem them very highly in love because of their work."
1 Thessalonians 5:12-14 (ESV)

"Remember your leaders, those who spoke to you the word of God. Consider the outcome of their way of life, and imitate their faith."
Hebrews 13:7 (ESV)

For the past several years, I've been privileged to be a member of Coach's Edge, an "applied learning community" founded and led by Cheryl Scanlan, MCC. In late 2022, I realized that in this community I had grown not only in my coaching competence but also in my character. While being taught the "what" and "how" of coaching by Cheryl, I also caught the "who" of the coach simply by being in her presence and with other members of our community. For example, while we were debriefing a coaching demonstration of Cheryl's, she admitted, "I didn't catch that," and followed with, "I'm still working on that." We learned many skills in that demo, but we also deeply experienced her gracious humility.

God impressed on me quite strongly that it wasn't enough for me to privately notice Cheryl's ongoing contribution to our character—her investment needed to be publicly affirmed and appreciated. He graciously planted a seed in my heart and mind to join Him in creating something beautiful that would bless and encourage both Cheryl and those in the wake of her influence. Over the past several months, it's been my privilege to form and lead a team to write a book about the character of the Christian coach.

Learning about agreements, awareness, and action is critical in the formation of a coach, but it is not enough to know what to do and how to do it. Our *doing*—demonstrating skills, using various techniques and tools, and so on—flows from the depths of our *being*. While we all heartily affirm the importance of growing in our coaching, this book invites you to explore the character that undergirds your competence. It is our aim to help you notice the importance of *who you are* as a coach and encourage you to be intentional in developing your character.

Before I summarize how the book is organized, I need to unpack a term you'll encounter often in the pages that follow—a term coined by Cheryl. When you read the term "off-roader," you'll probably envision someone emerging from a decked-out Jeep, splattered with mud and wearing a big grin! And that's *almost* what we mean when "translated" to the context of professional-grade coaching. Off-roader coaches not only honor the essence of the International Coaching Federation (ICF) core competencies, more importantly, they also are led by the Holy Spirit in their coaching partnerships. As such, off-roaders will demonstrate professional coaching skills (i.e., "drive on the road") *and* understand that the Spirit may lead them to engage with even greater skill (i.e., "drive on a rocky, rugged trail with a stream crossing"), depending on what is in their client's best interest at the moment. This does not mean "going rogue" (e.g., being unethical), but instead being comfortable with creativity and nuance in the moment.

When you turn the page, you'll find 13 chapters covering distinct character qualities essential to an off-roading coach. While each chapter is short, it has the potential for significant impact (yes, we learned this from Cheryl also)! The character qualities are in alphabetical order, conveying that no one quality is more important than the others; frankly, we would argue that the qualities are mutually supportive. Some chapters are interviews I held with a fellow coach; others are self-contained essays. In each chapter, you'll explore the meaning and impact of a coaching character quality. That is, you'll appreciate what it's like to receive the quality from a coach, and you'll grasp the impact on your clients when you "give" this quality to them. At the end of each chapter, we invite you to engage with questions that will help you "explore the off-road" so you can grow in that quality.

This book was written by coaches, for coaches, so we invite you to take a "coach approach" as you read the book. In cooperation with the Holy Spirit, we encourage you to set an intention for growth before you begin. Since character is forged in community, we also challenge you to invite another coach (or coaches) to join you on your journey. The developmental questions at the end of each chapter are tailored for engaging with others, and the invitational chapter at the end of the book was also written for this purpose. May God be glorified, and may this book be life-giving to you!

— Scott Frickenstein, April 2023, Fernandina Beach, Florida

CALLED
Scott Frickenstein

"We have become His poetry, a re-created people that will fulfill the destiny He has given each of us, for we are joined to Jesus, the Anointed One. Even before we were born, God planned in advance our destiny and the good works we would do to fulfill it!"
Ephesians 2:10 (TPT)

It is natural for humans to wonder "what on earth am I here for?" The theological concept of calling (vocation) explores this terrain. Secular organizations inadvertently attest to this important biblical framework: Monster.com beckoned, "Your calling is calling,"[1] and Gallup hosts a "Called to Coach" webcast.[2] Let's explore what it means to be called and the implications of calling for coaches and their clients.

Much has been written about what it means to be "called,"

and a comprehensive resource review is provided in the notes.[3] In sum, the secular worldview equates "calling" with choosing a career and champions the desires of the one making that choice. The biblical perspective, on the other hand, acknowledges a Caller who invites individuals to play their part in His larger story. Martin Luther beautifully explained calling as God's means of providentially directing and caring for His creatures.

A Christian's primary calling is to *be* God's own; each one's secondary callings are everything they *do* in response to their primary calling. By saying coaches are called, we mean that God has summoned them and is preparing them to partner with the Holy Spirit in their clients' personal and professional transformation (in a way that is distinctly different from that of a counselor, consultant, or mentor). That's the theory—now let's discover what a called coach looks like in practice.

After spending a nanosecond with Cheryl, you'd have a strong sense that she has been called by God—first to Himself and then to love her family and impact the world through coaching. Based on her identity in Christ, Cheryl models two clear callings: to come alongside her clients in their transformation and to raise up many excellent coaches. She constantly and enthusiastically expresses the conviction that coaching is deeply needed now—especially in the Church— and that coaching is having enormous ripple effects in the lives of individuals, their families, and their organizations. While Cheryl educates members of her Coach's Edge community, she exudes both delight and a seriousness that the stakes are high—concurrently conveying that what we are learning is fun and that applying it really matters.

Called coaches experience both joyful freedom and purposefulness as they cooperate with the Holy Spirit in coming alongside their clients. In *Chariots of Fire*, Eric Liddell famously said, "When I run, I feel His pleasure." It's exhilarating to see God bring a client awareness in a session and transform a client through a coaching partnership. And when a client says something like, "That's a really good question—I've never thought about that" or "No one has ever noticed that before!" or "God is using our partnership to change so many aspects of my life," the called coach indeed "feels God's pleasure." But called coaches also feel the weight of the role God has invited them to play; they have a burden, not merely a career or an occupation. Thus, called coaches wholeheartedly understand they must—not merely "should" or "could"—coach.

In addition to joy and "weightiness," there are several other implications of being a called coach. First, called coaches are ① grounded in knowing God led them into coaching. This notion of being called is especially poignant for coaches, since coaching is typically not their first professional undertaking—they trusted God's leading from what was familiar into uncharted territory. As such, the second implication of called coaches is humble dependence on God for every aspect of their work; they are fully aware that "this is bigger than me!" ② Third, this call fosters a sense of stewardship—a commitment to intentionally prepare and "sharpen their edge" by pursuing ③ education, training, and mentoring. Finally, coaches remember that all callings are opposed and often entail some undesirable aspects. But the perspective that "God called me to this" ④ motivates coaches to (1) remember their God-given "high point" moments, (2) seek assistance for any aspects of being a coach that may not seem life-giving (e.g., networking, marketing, bookkeeping, etc.), and (3) "stay the course" (e.g., Nehemiah 6:3). We now turn to the impact of each coach's calling on his or her clients.

Each coach's calling is both visible and palpable for his or her clients. Since God is working through the called coach to transform the client, the client of a called coach will first know that he or she is in good hands. Early in their partnership it will become clear to the client that his or her coach is a skilled professional who really enjoys working with the client—he or she is being served as someone created in the image of God, not treated like a number. Second, the client of a called coach will also be able to rest in noticing his or her coach's impeccable ethics (e.g., confidentiality) in ways unlike what he or she may have experienced in other settings. Third, the client will feel that his or her coach is truly "for me"; the coach isn't merely collecting payment nor passing time—something, actually Someone greater is at work in their coaching partnership. I have truly been blessed in these ways as the client of a coach who has been clearly called by God.

There is a deep sense of God's design and purposefulness—indeed, a weight—in a calling to coach. But coaches also experience joy as they partner with God in the work of transforming a client's life. Clients of called coaches can settle into a life-changing partnership, knowing their coach is truly *for* them; over time, clients will also notice their coach exhibiting the qualities explored in upcoming chapters.

For Your Off-Road Journey:

- ❖ What is your "call to coaching" story?
- ❖ What have you noticed about someone who is called to coach?
- ❖ What other implications of a coach's calling come to mind?

❖ What is your "go to" when your sense of calling is stalled or directly challenged?

End Notes

1. https://www.youtube.com/watch?v=Xam7Dws_UfU accessed on 1/30/2023.
2. https://www.gallup.com/topic/coachwebcast.aspx accessed on 1/30/2023.
3. Frickenstein, Scott. The Concept of "Calling" and Its Relevance to the Military Professional. BiblioScholar, 2012 (ISBN 1286863694).

CALMING
Doreen Steenland

"Be still, and know that I am God."
Psalm 46:10 (ESV)

Imagine a calm, tranquil lake, the water glistening in the sun. The brightness blinds your naked eyes. You breathe in a long and steady breath of relaxation as you settle in to BE present in this very moment. You hear birds chirping as they rustle in the trees overhead. Your senses sharpen to listen and notice. You see an occasional ripple in the water from a hungry fish surfacing as they capture their prey; the ripple spreads over the water and then silently leaves the scene. A family of ducks join in, slowly gliding across the water. Their movement is effortless, and they swim together as if an invisible rope links them. They start on the surface and then gently dip their heads below the surface to look at what is below. These ducks, like coach and client, remain together, present in the calm and engaged in the beautiful exploration that is before them.

This visual presents a metaphor of the partnership between a coach and client. Some clients swoop in like an eagle, looking to snatch their prey from the tranquil waters to become their evening meal. Others come from a place of gliding, surveying the landscape, uncertain of where the next satisfying nugget of nourishment will appear. The constant is the coach's presence. The coach is to BE a space of calm, curious, and stabilizing energy for the client that, like a breath of fresh air, empowers them to inhale the unseen possibilities that exist in their lives.

The coach is called to embody a calm, non-anxious presence. The term "non-anxious presence," originally coined by Jewish Rabbi and family therapist Edwin Friedman, is used to describe an individual who provides a calm, cool, focused, and collected environment that empowers others to be relaxed.[2] Being in a place of non-anxious attachment allows us to be present with, but not consumed by our client's stories. This calmness activates a spirit of curiosity and exploration that enables us to show up powerfully for our clients. The ICF Core Competencies of "Embodies a Coaching Mindset" and "Maintains Presence" describe this in various ways.

The off-roader does not become calm by inactivity but by intentional engagement of their whole self in connection with God and the client. This is a posture of *being* versus *doing*. The intentionality begins with the coach, with forethought of the client and self-management of his or her own inner and outer worlds. This calming presence is activated in a region of the brain that is full of possibility, non-judgmental curiosity, and big picture thinking with God.

Calmness comes from a state of abiding in Christ, listening carefully to His voice and one's intuition, as well as the ability to regulate one's own shifting emotions. This posture enables coaches to listen for what is not being spoken with words so they can help the client access the deep waters of their heart and draw them out (Proverbs 20:5). Without this calming presence, one misses many opportunities to travel to the depths of the soul. Off-roaders go to the depths. As Thoreau has said, "You cannot perceive beauty, but with a serene mind."[3]

There is a sacred partnership between the calm coach, God, and the client. Self-regulation is an important aspect of maintaining this calming characteristic in an off-roader. The distraction of your internal emotions can become a barricade to partnership; therefore, the coach must deliberately maintain inner calm. Cheryl once said ducks look peaceful and calm on top of the water but are often paddling furiously underneath it.[4]

Off-roaders are aware of their inner battles and have the tools to return quickly to a calm space. A gentle focus on one's breath can provide the anchor for runaway thoughts and feelings. While a frenzy of inner turmoil robs us of clarity, laser focus, and curiosity due to their location in the brain, slowing down our breathing allows us to self-regulate, regain mastery of our attention, and return to harmony. This empowers us to bounce back to our higher-level brain function and a calm connection with our client and God.

Reclaiming calm opens many avenues for a coach to explore with a client. The best questions and observations come from a quiet spirit and the deep well of a heart that is calm and grounded. A calming presence opens the coach's and client's minds to find the answers that already exist within them. William Burroughs serves us well when he reminds us that, "Your mind will answer most questions if you learn to relax and wait for the answers."[5]

Off-roaders stand as a calm presence, holding a sacred space for their clients to discover their own internal treasures.

For Your Off-Road Journey:

❖ What have you noticed about your state of calm in your coaching?

❖ When have you noticed leaving your calming space during a coaching session?

❖ What did that departure from connection expose for you?

End Notes:

1. https://ct.counseling.org/2018/06/five-pragmatic-tools-to-become-a-nonanxious-presence-tips-and-tricks-for-being-a-mindful-counselor/

2. https://www.mattnorman.com/non-anxious-leadership/

3. Henry David Thoreau.

4. "Be like a duck. Calm on the surface, but always paddling like the dickens underneath." Michael Caine.

5. William S. Burroughs.

CO-CREATIVE
A Conversation with Mark Ross,

"He's the one who comforts us in all our trouble so that we can comfort other people who are in every kind of trouble. We offer the same comfort that we ourselves received from God."
2 Corinthians 1:4 (CEB)

The International Coaching Federation defines coaching as "partnering with clients in a thought-provoking and creative process that inspires them to maximize their personal and professional potential." Mark Ross and I explored this character quality of co-creative because it so powerfully undergirds the partnership a coach establishes with their client. We invite you to listen in on our invigorating discussion of the freedom, beauty and "seismic shifts" this quality brings to coaches and clients.

not "I have the answers"

What does it mean to be co-creative?

Being co-creative means coming alongside. The verse above paints a beautiful picture of what it looks like when someone is going through a hard time. But we can also come alongside someone who is going through an important time. Unlike a "sage on the stage," being co-creative can mean coming alongside your client and sharing in areas where you may be a little further along in your journey. At other times, it may mean a time of agreeing to collaborate on ideas that serve clients outside your realm of experience.

What's especially life-giving for you about being co-creative?

Being co-creative reduces the potential for intimidation because it is an invitation to create something together. If clients are supported in taking the lead, it can result in powerful ideas and solutions that serve them well. This way, one plus one may become more than the sum of its parts, which is way more exciting!

What story comes to mind when you think about being co-creative?

Cheryl was always co-creative as my mentor coach. During one session, she invited me to watch a video and said, "I think this will resonate with you." She had noticed something in me that I hadn't understood yet. When we talked about the video, it helped me distinguish between adventuring and exploring, which are two very nuanced ways of being. Cheryl's coming alongside me in a co-creative way was helpful and encouraging. I remember it vividly because it wasn't a solution just handed to me. We worked in partnership.

What makes being co-creative essential for a coach?
Being co-creative is the heartbeat of a coaching partnership. Consider the ICF core competencies, which define professional-grade coaching. Being co-creative supports the competencies of "Establishes and Maintains Agreements," "Cultivates Trust and Safety," "Maintains Presence," and so on. I don't think you can be an effective coach without being co-creative.

What's different about you because co-creativity has been modeled for you?
When I began my coaching journey seven years ago, I had more of a consultant mindset. Being co-creative has helped me listen at a deeper level to identify what's really happening in the conversation. As a visual artist, I occasionally introduce new colors into my work. Being co-creative provides a new "color palette" to help me work in the heart, soul, and mind of my clients—to notice what matters most. I now have a richer life experience and look at life's challenges and opportunities through the lens of a coach, which brings me confidence and encouragement. That's exciting!

What do you notice in you as someone is co-creating with you?
I notice that space is being held for me to think before I speak. Co-creating invites me to go deeper, exploring possibilities before I've voiced them, and I don't feel like someone's waiting on me to provide the answer. I feel like someone is pacing with me to find the best answers without telling me their opinion. Sometimes it's gentle: "Would you like to explore some ideas together that you might want to consider as you move forward and see what surfaces?" Other times it's very direct. During a

co-creative moment in our coaching partnership a while back, Cheryl asked, "Mark, what's it going to take for things to shift for you?" That was seismic, but not in terms of shame. It helped because Cheryl was able to bring out the best in me.

What impact does being co-creative have in other aspects of your life?

Being co-creative is shaping how I approach the teaching ministry in my church. I often pause during the lesson and ask, "What's coming up for you so far? What are you thinking? If you walked out right now, what difference would it make?" Being co-creative is making me a better artist, husband, and father. Additionally, being co-creative is building my confidence. Instead of being intimidated about what to say while engaging with someone in a high-impact position, I am simply curious about them and ask a few curious questions about their life and work.

Being co-creative is touching everything about you! What difference is it making in your coaching?

After my initial coach training, I felt quite constrained. But I've learned that I can honor the coaching competencies while taking risks and trying new things. Being co-creative gives me freedom to approach each client differently—based on their personality, our agreement, and so on—so I manage a co-creative experience that best serves them. Being co-creative is making coaching much more enjoyable, exciting, and energizing than it was in the beginning.

You sense a lot of freedom knowing there are "mechanics" to good coaching, but good coaches don't have to be "mechanical." As a creator of beauty in many

different contexts, painting being one of those, what beauty are you seeing God create in your coaching through being co-creative?

In my heart of hearts, I'm an artist. When I make a visual image, the result is often different than what I intended because God co-creates beauty with me along the way. When I coach, God co-creates beauty as people move toward what matters most to them.

What would be different if you were not co-creative in your coaching?

If I were not co-creative, clients would not work with me very long because we wouldn't establish much of a relationship; trust wouldn't be earned nor experienced. The client wouldn't see change over time, and they would likely not perceive much value. It would be a frustrating journey that neither of us would enjoy.

Mark, what would you share with our readers to bring this all together?

Coaching is not therapy, but it can be therapeutic. Coaching is not consulting, but it can be consultative. For me, coaching is an advanced form of encouragement. When I work with my coach, I receive a "spiritual massage." The heartbeat of that relationship is the co-creative experience of trust, presence, and the sense of invitation.

For Your Off-Road Journey:

❖ What are some things you're doing now to grow in being co-creative?
  ➤ What's working?
  ➤ What's not working?

- ❖ Have you considered listening to Cheryl's coaching demonstrations to witness co-creativity in action?
- ❖ Have you considered becoming part of a coaching community where coaching skills are honed?

COMPASSIONATE
A Conversation with Kathleen Fischer

*"Praise be to the God and Father of our Lord Jesus
Christ, the Father of compassion and the God of all
comfort."*
2 Corinthians 1:3 (NIV)

In our volatile and complex world, we all know what it is
like to suffer alone, and thus, we deeply appreciate someone
who will enter into our suffering. Kathleen Fischer and I
probed how being compassionate has impacted her life and
transformed her coaching. Deepening your understanding of
this beautiful character quality will help you gently come
alongside your clients when you notice they are suffering.

What does it mean to be compassionate?
Merriam-Webster defines compassion as "sympathetic
consciousness of others' distress, together with a desire to

alleviate it." God often describes himself as compassionate. In our epigraph, we see that God's compassion is expressed through the comfort He brings to us, even if He doesn't necessarily take our troubles away. In Matthew 14, Jesus was hurting after hearing about the death of his precious cousin, John the Baptist, so he withdrew to be alone in a boat. But the crowds followed Him; when He came ashore, "He had compassion on them and healed them," putting their needs above His own. In these examples we see two different ways that God shows compassion. One was with His comfort in the midst of distress, while the second was to remove distress by solving the problem. God is perfect in His wisdom as He discerns how to best show compassion.

What stories come to mind when you think about being compassionate?

Cheryl immediately comes to mind when I think about compassion. I don't think there has ever been a Coach's Edge call where I have not seen Cheryl demonstrate the character quality of compassion as she nurtures those she is leading. Cheryl created Coach's Edge out of her compassion. She was sympathetically conscious of the struggles one can experience when building a coaching business, and she sought to alleviate those struggles by creating a community so we didn't have to be alone. Members of her community are comforted through fellowship in their journey, while they also gain confidence in their coaching skills and the additional training credits needed for further certifications. During COVID, Cheryl also went above and beyond by offering additional opportunities to connect and pray together so we weren't suffering in isolation. This was another demonstration of her gracious, self-sacrificial compassion as a coaching leader.

What makes being compassionate essential for a coach?
Being compassionate is essential for a coach because it brings us into the sacred space of caring for the whole person instead of only their agenda. For example, while establishing the agenda for a call, the client shared a struggle she was having with one of her children. I perceived she was experiencing acute pain in that relationship; she was suffering. Moments like this are critical for coaches. A coach's compassion might stimulate a desire to dive into the issue or try to solve it. But Cheryl has taught us to observe and then discern what is in the client's best interest. That may mean being silent and letting it be or opening space to allow the client to shift the agenda to address it, and so on.

What does the client want? In this case, I shared my observation that she seemed to be experiencing a high level of pain regarding her child. She affirmed my observation. Knowing that this client valued prayer, I asked if she would like me to pray for her in that moment. She said, "Yes. Please." So I briefly prayed for her. It was interesting to see the level of reaction my client had when she let out a deep sigh at the end of the prayer and then expressed the depth of relief she felt. In turn, she felt freed up to move back into the work of her original agenda.

In your compassion, you noticed her pain and gave her the option of what to do with what you noticed. Your alignment with "the Father of compassion" opened up **some things for the rest of the call.**
Yes! It did. As coaches, being compassionate requires creating a safe space for the client to decide what he or she wants to do. They may express personal pain as we start working on a

business issue, but a coaching call may not be the space to address it. As we observe their suffering and have the desire to alleviate it, we must trust the Holy Spirit to help us create a space that allows the client to decide what is best.

Recently, there was another client who wanted to work on shifting the way she was working. As she shared, she mentioned that her husband was halfway around the world, and she had just received a troubling medical diagnosis. She was suffering with fear and loneliness in his absence but believed her diagnosis may be tied to her desired agenda, so she wanted to stay focused on that. In turn, we did not address her suffering directly.

After our call, I was reminded of Cheryl's invitation to be off-roaders, so I prayed for an appropriate way to help relieve her suffering. I knew this client liked worship music, so the next day I sent her a worship song and a devotion to encourage her. My client wrote back these words: "You have no idea how much it means to know that you are standing with me right now."

My decision to take a risk to show that I was not just "with her in her business" but was with her in her suffering, ended up bringing her the compassion she needed. Coaches have an incredible privilege to be God's "hands and feet" as we embody compassion to our clients.

What would be different for your clients if you were not compassionate?

If I was not compassionate, my clients would miss out on being wholly coached, which is something Cheryl often refers to. If I was solely focused on a client's stated agenda, I could miss the impact their personal suffering is having on that agenda. When I prayed with the client I mentioned earlier, she remembered God is bigger than her struggle and is present with her in it. That released her to fully engage with me on her original agenda. Without becoming sympathetically conscious of a client's suffering and being open to the best way to show compassion, a client's suffering could remain unaddressed and festering below the surface, ultimately hindering their forward movement on the agendas that really matter to them.

When you offer your clients the gift of compassion, focusing on them as whole people and not only on their circumstantial problems, you are bringing them "with-ness." This reminds me of how the three-letter prefix "com" in compassion is loaded with importance.

Yes! Being compassionate as a coach means entering into the suffering *with* a client while managing our desire to alleviate it. That with-ness is a powerful way to bring comfort in their distress. But it also requires more from us than simply being empathetic (feeling what they feel). It requires us to resist being caught up in their pain and to be disciplined enough to come alongside our clients from the heart in ways that are truly in their best interest.

What would you share with our readers to bring this all together?

I believe being compassionate allows us to be the hands and feet of God. It is costly, yet powerful. It allows us the sacred privilege of experiencing the heart of God who suffers with us in our pain yet applies His wisdom in discerning what is best for us. It allows us to truly serve our clients out of the heart of God.

For Your Off-Road Journey:

- ❖ When have you become "sympathetically conscious" of a client's distress?
- ❖ What did you do with that observation?
- ❖ How willing are you to be self-sacrificial as you observe a client in their pain?
- ❖ What would it look like for you to lean into God for His discernment and help in such cases?
- ❖ How would the outcome of God's help impact you personally?

COMPETENT
A Conversation with Cindy Schmelzenbach

"Show yourself in all respects to be a model of good works, and in your teaching show integrity, dignity."
Titus 2:7 (ESV)

My interview with Cindy Schmelzenbach expanded my thinking on this character quality. Her perspective on being competent as a way of humbly honoring God, our clients, and ourselves inspired me to continue "raising my game" and to go "Beyond Competence" as our book declares. Let's explore what it means to be competent and the impact our competence has on our coaching.

What does being competent mean to you?
Being competent is often defined in terms of capability, that is, having the ability, knowledge, or skill needed to do something successfully. But being competent means so much more to me—it's a way of showing honor. To show up having put forth effort is a way of showing my clients that they matter and are worth my effort. Competency is as much about my approach as it is about the result—it's an indication of my dedication, my humility, and my gratitude.

What about being competent inspires you?
For me, growing in competence is my response to God's invitation into a sacred partnership. Doing my part to grow in my skills—and the mindset that aligns with those skills—allows me to be more open to seeing and participating in God's invitation.

What makes being competent essential for a coach?
We owe it to our fellow coaches to pursue and demonstrate competence, since the reputation of our profession is helped or hurt by each coach's demonstration of competency. We also owe it to ourselves. The first thing we can do to win the battle against a lack of confidence is to become competent. Most of all, we owe it to our clients. It's unethical and dishonorable for me to offer my services as a coach without having put forth the work and met the standards to do it well.

What is different about you because Cheryl has modeled being competent?
One of my core values is excellence, so I'm attracted to competence. Cheryl models such a beautiful blend of humility and competence in the way she coaches, teaches, and leads. She

has helped me to see that my competence is something I can affect, and then leave the results of my coaching up to God. My competence is also my offering, an indication of how much I value the partnerships I am invited into. I have a sacred opportunity to honor my clients through my pursuit of ever-increasing competence.

What do you notice as you experience someone being competent?

When I'm with a professional that demonstrates competence, I experience safety; I know I'm being seen and heard with professional care. As the client of a competent coach, I don't have to "carry their side of the partnership," worrying if I've clearly articulated everything. I can relax and enjoy the coaching process, trusting my proficient partner. I don't have to do their work for them! In every interaction I've had with Cheryl, she has brought her whole life experience to bear. I feel honored by that.

How is being competent impacting you as a coach?

Being competent helps me when I struggle with imposter syndrome—something we all wrestle with as coaches. It also grows my faith, as I'm much bolder to ask God to take my offering and make something out of it that only He can do. Being competent also increases my gratitude. It's a great gift knowing that I can fully participate in the work God is doing in the life of a client and that I can do that with intentionality and diligence.

What does being competent bring to other aspects of your life?

I think we've got to keep competence in its rightful place. If I prove my competence in an area (indicated by a list of credentials, for example) and lack some of the other character qualities we've been discussing, I'll probably lack in my effectiveness as a professional. My *doing* would be impacted by my lack of *being*! On the flip side, my *being* can catalyze growth in my *doing*. And my competence will positively impact each of the other qualities. But even then, sometimes God invites me into a context where I do not feel competent. In those cases, I rely on Him even more; I need to be willing to be vulnerable and take risks, trusting Him with the outcome.

What does being competent bring to your coaching?
Being competent means I have specific tools that I know have been developed and proven. That gives me a starting place. It makes me feel more willing to try new approaches or develop my own tools because I know I'm building on a solid foundation.

What does being competent open up for your clients?
If I'm competent, my clients have a sense of safety with me. This allows them to relax and be creative, knowing I'm competently "standing guard" over the process.

What beauty does God create in your coaching through your being competent?
God creates with competency. He invites me to experience this co-creative participation with Him as He does all things well. God also creates beauty as I honor our partnership by bringing my competence to my clients.

What would be different for your clients if you were not competent?

If I were not competent, I don't think I would have any clients! And it wouldn't be right for me to expect to have any clients. Attending to professional competency is the first action step I can take before I ask for the opportunity to partner with a client in a coaching relationship. It's also something that is never complete. I don't have to be perfect or reach a specific competency standard to be on a journey with clients; instead, I'm always seeking to better serve and honor them by increasing my competence.

What would you share with our readers to bring this all together?
Competency is a virtue that we can know we are attending to and growing in. So many of the virtues are internally measured and can be a challenge to evaluate. But we can measure coaching competence; we can gain external validation. We can take intentional steps to grow in our competence, so why wouldn't we? Being competent honors God, our clients, and ourselves.

For Your Off-Road Journey:

* ❖ What would be different if you had 10% more competence?

* ❖ What tiny habit will catalyze your growth in competence?

* ❖ What opportunities are available to increase your competence?

* ❖ Where can you see intentional steps you have taken that resulted in increased competence?

* ❖ What does competence free you up to experience more of?

COURAGEOUS
Todd Kemp

Be willing to be fired.
Cheryl Scanlan

As I walked into Ted's office for our coaching session, I had barely closed the door when he launched into a rant that relentlessly spanned about twenty minutes. I sat listening and reflecting, figuratively holding a container for him to vent his frustrations into that afternoon. While his irritations over his employees, business partner, and teenage son had been building over the previous couple of months, this outburst seemed to be different, and not just in degree. As we explored his energy around this, I sensed a nudge from the Holy Spirit that He wanted me to give a specific message to Ted; I also felt this would be high risk.

There wouldn't be many natural openings in this conversation, so I leaned in toward Ted while he was still fuming over the transgressions of his employees. I shifted my arms onto his desk between us and laced my fingers together in a steepling posture to signal a shift in the conversation. "Ted," I said, activating a focused and purposeful way of *being* to command his attention. He paused and tilted his head upward slightly to meet my eyes with his own steely gaze. I asked as directly as I could, "Are you open to hearing an observation?"

"Yeah," he replied curtly.

"It seems like you're checked out. Checked out from your employees, your relationship with your partner, and from your business." I paused for a moment to allow Ted to absorb the shock waves. Then I added, "And it seems like you're checked out at home, too."

A powerful silence reigned for the next minute or two as I allowed space for Ted to process what he'd just heard. While I had built considerable relational capital with him in our coaching relationship over the previous couple of years, I wasn't entirely sure he might not come across his desk and take a swing at me or fire me on the spot. Nevertheless, I felt God's peace in having faithfully delivered the message so Ted could receive it.

Cheryl was not physically in the room with me that day, but her voice was in my head as I sat listening to Ted that afternoon. "Be willing to be fired" were the words that rang clear to me in that moment. Cheryl has shared this mantra with us, and it sprung to life for me that day. In other words, she might say, "Be courageous to say what you're seeing without attachment, and let the client decide what to do with it. Go dance on the edge of your comfort zone and your client's, because that's where great coaching happens and transformation begins—yours and theirs." Read that again and imagine Cheryl saying this in the moment. I'm sure those who know her see her face, hear her clarity, feel her sense of conviction and urgency, and hear her "y'all" tacked on to give us one more measure of loving encouragement. It's so good, isn't it?!

To show up as a courageous coach is to engage with clarity, conviction, and urgency for the sake of those we coach and for the Kingdom. In partnership with the Holy Spirit, courageous coaches pray expectantly, listen extravagantly, and look earnestly for what God might be doing in, around, and through our clients. This brings clarity and conviction. And then there comes a time when, with humility and courage, we step into the moment and speak a word that might change the course of a conversation, a way of believing, and a way of living. That is the courageous coaching moment! "Courage," C.S. Lewis wrote, "is not simply one of the virtues but the form of every virtue at the testing point."[1] Courage is required to create breakthrough moments. Since such moments are often fleeting, we dare not miss them. Scripture reminds us that the time we're given is short. "You are a mist that appears for a little while and then vanishes" (James 4:14, NIV). A courageous coach, therefore, doesn't postpone saying what needs to be said. Living in the precious present, we come to realize that now is the only time we have to make a difference. We've been called to be courageous coaches—to bring sharp, discerning clarity, the conviction of the Holy Spirit, and "the fierce urgency of now."[2]

Courage would not be needed if we didn't experience fear. Cheryl says fear is at the core of our resistance to step into a critical moment, which is rooted in an identity crisis and connected to a type of idol or an unbelief.[3] She encourages us to "recognize and root out fear" and notes that "fear is a weapon formed against us, and we get to decide whether we give it power."[4] This calls for courageous soul work as we acknowledge and press into the fear that lurks in the shadows. While the greatest commandments in Scripture are to love God and love our neighbor as ourselves, the most frequently cited directive is "Do not be afraid!" Note the connection the Apostle John makes between fear and love: "There is no fear in love. But perfect love drives out fear" (1 John 4:18, NIV). Cheryl suggests a question for us to bring before the Lord: "Where am I not understanding perfect love?"[5] Having examined our hearts with curiosity and compassion for ourselves, our task in becoming courageous coaches is to let go of the unbelief, receive God's perfect love—both for ourselves and our client—and allow Him to be larger than our fear. In so doing, we exchange a lie for the truth, displace fear with love, and make space for courageous living.

Being on the other side of a person who leans in courageously is life-giving. I am inspired, uplifted, strengthened, and free to join God anew in what He's up to in the world. Through another's courage, I can see more clearly through the fog of my confusion, overcome inertia, embrace the truth of God's love, and take courageous action. I become more of who God says I am.

Returning to the coaching session with Ted stewing in his thoughts in the long, awkward silence, his countenance softened. He eventually replied, "I think you're absolutely right. It's hard to hear it, but I think you're right. In fact, my daughter said something like that to me the other day. Thank you." I asked what he wanted to do with it, and he said he was going home early to talk with his wife about it. A month later at our next coaching session, Ted was like a new man, greeting me with a smile, a hug, and a brighter outlook on life, family, and work. He had done some soul-searching and had initiated some critical conversations. When others experience us being courageous, as Ted did, they experience greater clarity as well as hope, vitality, and renewed purpose.

The invitation for us as Christians is to step further into the abundant life Jesus came to give us (John 10:10) in the here and now, and this includes in our work as coaches. As we do, we get to draw others toward experiencing more of the good, true, and beautiful life Jesus offers. To live and coach courageously is a posture, a way of being that calls us and those we coach into this abundance. Being courageous is one aspect of Cheryl's character that distinguishes her as an exceptional coach, and I'm grateful for her modeling it well and calling us into it. It has made a tremendous difference in me and therefore for those I am privileged to coach.

For Your Own Off-Road Journey:

❖ Where does fear or anxiety show up for you in coaching or in life?

➤ What do you notice about it?

➤ What's the lie you're believing that's hijacking you?

➤ What's the truth?

➤ What do you need to let go of?

➤ How might you replace it and receive more of God's love for you in that?

❖ Recall a recent situation where fear hijacked you. Now imagine a new, yet similar upcoming situation, and this time you have clarity on what's true, you're embracing God's love more fully, and you act and speak with greater courage.

- ➤ What's that like for you?
- ➤ What shift might that create for you as a coach?
- ➤ For the people you coach?
- ➤ What step could you take to show up with greater courage in the days ahead?

End Notes:

1. Lewis, C.S. *The Screwtape Letters.* Scribner, 1982.
2. King, M.L., Jr. https://www.marshall.edu/onemarshallu/i-have-a-dream/, accessed 3/9/2023.
3. Scanlan, Cheryl. Coach's Edge Advanced Skill Mastery event, Nov. 11, 2020.
4. Ibid.
5. Ibid.

DEEPLY ATTUNED
Pamela Mertz

Powerful questions come from powerful listening.
Cheryl Scanlan

If we could distill the essence of an off-roader coach's character into two words, they would be "deeply attuned." Let's explore what it means to be deeply attuned, what it's like to interact with someone who is deeply attuned to you, and what being deeply attuned brings to our clients.

Merriam-Webster defines "attuned" as "aware of and attentive or responsive to something."[1] Attuned is often paired with the word "to," meaning being attentive and responsive in a certain direction or toward something specific. An off-roader coach is deeply attuned to their client, to the Holy Spirit, and to themselves.

Cheryl has masterfully modeled all three facets of this

character quality for me. When I engage with her, I immediately sense that I am being fully noticed. Cheryl has prepared for our time and is "dialed in" to my energy, my demeanor, my emotions, and to what I say (and don't say) and how I say it. I experience a deep with-ness, a full partnership with her as we process something that matters to me. As Cheryl partners with me, she is listening ("in") to the Holy Spirit—not merely listening "to, for, and with" (e.g., for data, my nonverbals, tone). Her higher-level listening leads to rich exploration and, in turn, new awareness for me. Not only is Cheryl deeply attuned to me and to the Holy Spirit, she's also very attentive to herself. During a recent Coach's Edge live demonstration, she was experiencing intense pain and was fully aware of the impact it was having on her presence as a coach.

My clients experience deep transformation when I'm deeply attuned to them, the Holy Spirit, and myself. When I show up for a coaching session prepared and attentive, I catch a lot in the first few seconds, which we use in co-creating the session's coaching agenda (I even pick up gold nuggets beforehand if we open in prayer). My clients also benefit when I listen at deep levels to what is said, how it's said, and to what is not said. If I notice subtle shifts in cadence, tone, or emotion, I may ask, "What are you becoming aware of?" As I attune to the Holy Spirit, I often simply hold a sacred space of silence for my clients, allowing the Spirit to work in them as they marinate in their own thoughts and reflect on their own words.

When I notice a client beginning to gain clarity, I remain attuned, following their lead as they continue to hear and listen with me and the Holy Spirit. In our with-ness, my clients begin to settle into the process of coaching and gain traction. When my clients can turn their focus inward and God-ward, transformation begins to emerge, their traction increases, and significant revelation often occurs. They may exclaim, "This is a new way of looking at this!" or even, "Wow, this coaching thing really works!" It is a joy to remain attuned, reflecting and celebrating with them as new paths are created for their thoughts to travel upon.

Being attuned to yourself is the final dimension of how to best serve your clients. Know when you are at your peak, and honor yourself when you need to rest. If you are a morning person, do not offer evening coaching. You know yourself best; taking time to tend to you makes you more able to serve your clients well.

Being deeply attuned allows you to simultaneously partner with God and your client. Being intentionally present to your client, the Holy Spirit, and yourself enables you to serve your clients as you have been designed to. This work—this assignment—was created by God for you to carry out long before you entered the world (Ephesians 2:10).[3] *This* is Christian coaching that will bring the change that the world so desperately needs.

For Your Off-Road Journey:

* ❖ Think of a time when you felt heard—truly listened to.
  * ➤ What feelings are you aware of as you recall this?
  * ➤ What is welling up and becoming clear about yourself as you remember this?
* ❖ How would you want your clients to describe how you listen to them?
* ❖ When have you noticed that you were listening to make sure you could formulate that next, powerful question?
  * ➤ What did that feel like in the process of

coaching?

❖ How do you hear from God when you are coaching?

❖ What would help you practice this more and feel more attuned to Him as you coach?

❖ What does being attuned to yourself look like for you?

<u>End Notes:</u>

1. Merriam-Webster dictionary.

2. *Co-Active Coaching*, by Henry & Karen Kimsey-House, Phillip Sandahl, Laura Whitworth, and PCCI Essentials of Leadership Curriculum.

3. Ephesians 2:10, NASB: *"For we are His workmanship, created in Christ Jesus for good works, which God prepared beforehand so that we would walk in them."*

DIRECT
A Conversation with Kiley Lee

"'Martha, Martha', the Lord answered, 'you are
worried and upset about many things, but
few things or indeed are needed —
only one'..."
Luke 10:41-42 (NIV)

Coaches are very familiar with the skill of direct communication, but what character qualities give rise to this important behavior? Kiley Lee and I enjoyed an engaging conversation in which she unpacked the quality of being direct. Lean in and learn about a gift that "blows open doors" and requires a carefully set "dial."

What does it mean to you to be direct?
Coaches are engaged and attuned (both to self and the client)

so that they notice things. They have a courageous willingness to offer what is noticed to their client using straightforward language, and are humble, curious, and unattached to what the client does with what has been offered. Being direct is not the same as being blunt, which is being direct while disregarding someone's feelings. I like Adam Grant's quote: "Being direct with the content of your feedback doesn't prevent you from being thoughtful about the best way to deliver it."

What made "being direct" rise to the top out of all the qualities you appreciate most as a coach?

I don't know how you can be a coach without having some level of directness. Clarity is a way to show kindness; when done well, being direct offers a treasure that someone doesn't have access to on their own. Being direct entails trusting the relationship enough to share what you really think, allowing the conversation to go deep into the heart of the matter.

What scripture or quotes come to mind?

Jesus often shared very directly. He told Martha, "You are worried and upset about many things" (Luke 10:41, NIV), and Peter was "seeing things merely from a human point of view, not from God's" (Matthew 16:23, NLT). At a Coach's Edge event on direct communication, Cheryl said, "I want you to be able to speak boldly and unattached in a way that accelerates your clients' development; that is what keeps them coming back. You are trusting the relationship enough that you are willing to bring your observations to the table for them to evaluate any way they want to; this brings so much power to the conversation."

What do you notice in yourself when you receive someone's directness?

There are turning points in my life that took place because someone was direct with me—moments of illumination and insight that gave me the power of choice. Someone close to me once said, "You get an A plus for effort, but what you're doing isn't working and it's time to try something else." I could have gone to the depths of despair, but instead I used this as a jumping-off point to make difficult and costly life changes. I thank God for that conversation. When someone I trust is direct with me, I deeply value their statements more than any question they could ask me.

You feel enlightened and empowered when someone is direct with you, and know they sincerely want what's best for you.

Yes! I'm still reaping the benefits from Cheryl's demonstration of this quality. I had finished my coach training feeling like a bit of a hotshot and entered her mentor coaching practicum. After observing my coaching, she said, "You've nailed the technical skills, but I don't see Kiley in your coaching." It shocked me that there's a different standard outside the classroom! Coaching is not just about nailing the technical skills; there were questions I hadn't answered yet, such as "What does it mean to coach as myself?" "Who am I as a coach?" and "What is my style?"

All that from someone being direct with you … not intending to shame you, but to draw out the best in you.

That's when direct communication is beautiful.

And when someone is being direct with you, you change as you press into what they offer.
Being direct can be like showing me a door in my hallway that I didn't know was there. I open the door, and there's a new vista in front of me. Now I have a choice: Do I want to walk through the doorway or pass by and keep going down the hallway as originally intended? I still have the power of choice, but a new opportunity has been revealed.

What else do you notice in yourself when someone is direct with you?
It depends on if they're just being blunt! No one enjoys receiving, "Well, that's just the truth and if you can't handle it, that's your problem." But true directness always comes without attachment. Yes, it took courage for them to say something, but it must be coupled with humility in that they don't get to decide what I do with what they've said. It's up to me; they've released it to me as a gift.

So there's a hidden "dial" between "too direct" and "not direct enough"?
Yes. Cheryl has modeled "adjusting the dial" based on the recipient and how much trust is in the relationship. She's still Cheryl; she's still direct. But sometimes there is a softer delivery, and other times it is straight shooting, no fluff. Knowing there is a dial that needs to be adjusted is one of the biggest lessons I'm learning about this quality.

What does the gift of being direct—noticing something and doing something about it—bring to a client?
If you're just noticing, that's internal to you, and that might be

valuable. But there's something relational about choosing to offer what you noticed as a gift to your client.

Let's revisit the door in the hallway. Being direct may blow open more than one door down the hallway! It lets your clients see themselves in a different way—maybe a more accurate way—allowing their perspective to shift enough that new possibilities open up.

During a coaching demonstration, Cheryl asked a client, "What did you experience when I made that observation to you?" He said, "It was an invitation to seize clarity, to take hold of something instead of just sort of fumble." Cheryl replied, "That is the gift of direct communication—how clear it is." I imagine a blindfolded client, arms stretched in front and fumbling in the dark. Then someone removed the blindfold and put something tangible and weighty in his hand. He could choose to evaluate it or set it down, but he's not fumbling anymore; there's something to work with.

What beauty does God create when you bring this to your clients?
When I am direct with my clients, God accelerates their growth. He unleashes them to more quickly become who He created them to be and to do more of what He created them to do—because all of the fluff is stripped away faster. That's beautiful.

When you are direct, your clients experience the beauty of accelerated growth in their being and in their doing; without it, they fumble, as though a blindfold were on. What else would clients miss if you did not give them this gift?
It makes me sad to think about clients wasting time and money

on normal conversation! If I don't demonstrate the courage to offer something because it could possibly offend or disrupt them, they would miss out on opportunities that could benefit them. The client would miss excellence and hit mediocrity.

You mentioned you are learning to adjust your directness dial, and we discussed how a coach's courage and humility, along with the level of trust in the coaching partnership, help a coach adjust their level of directness. What else keeps your dial set correctly, somewhere between shrinking back and using a sledgehammer?
I also need a nonjudgmental, curious spirit, because I don't know how a client is going to receive my gift of directness. I don't know what they're going to do with it or its value to them.

It seems like *agape* love undergirds all these qualities; you want what's best for your client, regardless of the cost to yourself. If that means you need to be a little more courageous than you might normally be, you're willing to be that for their own good.
I got tears in my eyes when you said that. Sometimes people are surprised by my directness; and I continue to work on my own dial. But you have sensed my heart behind being direct: I don't want you to waste your energy on trying to read my mind or figure out what's important.

You show your cards instead of keeping them close to the vest.
I'm willing to be courageous on behalf of other people for their good—it's not to get things off my chest or to demand my own

way. My directness is rooted in a genuine desire to bring out the best in my clients.

What would you share with our readers as we conclude?
Be bold and courageous—without attachment— for the sake of your clients, and trust God with the outcome.

For Your Off-Road Journey:
- ❖ Begin with a self-assessment. On the continuum from indirect to direct, where do you typically set your directness dial?
- ❖ Where is God calling you to set it on behalf of your clients?
    - ➤ Paint a picture for yourself of where this is. What would it sound and feel like to set your dial there?
- ❖ How could you experiment with being more direct? Try some!
    - ➤ How did your experiments go?
    - ➤ What adjustments need to be made?
- ❖ What other steps can you take to grow in your skill of adjusting your dial?

GENUINE
A Conversation with Wende Gaikema

"Then Jesus said to the crowds and to his disciples, 'The scribes and the Pharisees sit on Moses' seat, so do and observe whatever they tell you, but not the works they do. For they preach, but do not practice'..."
Matthew 23:1-3 (ESV)

"Jesus wept."
John 11:35 (ESV)

In attempting to appreciate the depth of a character quality, it is sometimes helpful to first examine its opposite. The word "fake" typically engenders a visceral reaction in us—it seems we've all been negatively impacted by fake products and people. In this conversation, Wende Gaikema and I press into the importance of coaches being genuine.

What story comes to mind when you hear the word "genuine?"
In high school, I worked in the shops outside Pirates of the Caribbean in Disney World's Magic Kingdom. As I trained for this role in Disney University, they wanted us to be able to recognize counterfeit money, which was frequently passed in the park. I can still remember handling the counterfeit money and then holding and feeling real U.S. currency. The counterfeits often used lower quality paper and poor engraving, so it didn't feel quite right. Fake has a feel to it. In contrast, the real money was made of a unique paper that had thin strands of red and blue fiber in it and utilized precision engraving, so it had a certain "genuine" feel.

When I reflect on the quality of being genuine as a person and as a coach, it's similar in that when people aren't genuine, you feel it. Something's not quite right.

What does it mean to you to be genuine?
To be genuine is to be a whole and fully integrated person who has connected to his or her own values, emotions, strengths, and weaknesses without hubris or false humility. There is no arrogance. Genuine people are comfortable in their own skin and don't hide emotions. Jesus was genuine. Jesus wept (John 11:35), got angry (Matthew 21:12-13), and was moved with compassion (Mark 1:41). He wasn't afraid of His emotions, nor did they master Him; instead He expressed His emotions in service to others. Unlike the Pharisees, Jesus practiced what He preached.

Genuine people aren't working for the approval of others, as we see in Jesus' example when He spoke truth and did the right thing even when it clashed with the Pharisees (Matthew 23:1-36). He acted in a way consistent with His values; for example, healing on the Sabbath even though it was against Jewish law (Luke 6:6-11).

A genuine person can share their personal struggles with appropriate vulnerability, never making those struggles the center of attention but rather as a bridge to our common humanity. There is a consistency that creates safety as you know what you will get with this person. Genuine people are approachable, accepting and appreciative of others, and acknowledge that each person is valuable before God, with thoughts and ideas that are worthy to be heard. People are drawn to those who are genuine.

What does it feel like to be with someone who is genuine?
Genuine feels like a cozy winter night at home in your pajamas with a cup of hot chocolate in front of a crackling fire with your favorite people. Comfortable. Safe. Warm. Connected. No masks, so you can just be real.

Cheryl is this kind of person. As you work with her, you sense that she knows who she is in a calm and quiet way. She has a sincere interest in others, but out of loving curiosity, not being nosy. She acts with integrity, sharing her humanity while never making herself the focus. During one of our Coach's Edge calls, Cheryl shared that she was struggling with a headache and wasn't sure she could finish the call without being ill. That's genuine.

What do you notice as you experience someone being genuine?
This quality sets the table for deep connection. The genuine person creates safety for and invites vulnerability in others.

When you interact with a genuine person, you sense that they don't have a mask on. They are being their full, authentic self, which invites me in turn to show up with my full, authentic self.

As a result, I feel freedom, acceptance, warmth, and an openness in my body and spirit. Possibilities are created as I step into the light of who I am and who God created me to be. The Lord created us for relationship, and when I connect deeply in relationship as one genuine person to another, we create a conduit for the Holy Spirit to flow between us.

How is being genuine impacting you as a coach?

When Cheryl shares a window into some aspect of her life in a genuine and authentic way, I feel connected to her as a person and more committed to being open and genuine myself. Her appropriate vulnerability creates connection. As I experienced her being genuine with us, it challenged me to be my real self as I show up with my clients.

I believe it is a foundational prerequisite for creating a full coaching partnership—where two people connect soul to soul. In coaching, we often talk about "coaching the whole person." That is only truly possible when we first connect as one human being to another, without masks or pretense.

What does being genuine open up for your clients?

Coaches who are genuine help clients go further, faster, exploring depths, creating awareness, and enabling clarity and actions in areas that were previously murky. This is transformational, not transactional, coaching. Clients grow not just in what they do but in who they are. Clients are free to be who they are without judgment. Cheryl fully accepts her clients and our Coach's Edge group. Coming into the call with your whole person, warts and all, is not only accepted but encouraged. In today's culture there seem to be few places in life where you can safely be your genuine self and know that it's OK to show "all of you." Genuine people, such as Cheryl, create that space.

What does that look like in practice?

Vulnerability is appropriate, but there's a line that shouldn't be crossed. If the client asks how things are, you can tell them honestly but succinctly. You shouldn't tell long stories or go into detail as if you were talking to a friend. Coaches should show up as a real person with a real life but never take center stage. For instance, when Cheryl shares that she is in Tennessee and getting to see her granddaughter, we connect with her as a real person with real joys. When she uses a metaphor around fishing or how she fishes with her dad, we connect with her as a real person with a real story. When Cheryl must cancel an event because of a health issue, we connect with her as a real person with real struggles.

What does God create in your coaching through this quality?

Genuine Christian coaches reflect their Lord and Savior Jesus Christ when they show up as real people. Jesus was genuine. He shared His emotions and didn't pretend to be someone He wasn't. He was God incarnate—Emmanuel, "God with us." He said that plainly and clearly to those around Him. He could have tried to curry favor with the leading religious leaders of the time, but He didn't. In fact, He condemned their practices where He saw hypocrisy. We are called as believers to be a fragrant aroma of Him to those around us (2 Corinthians 2:15-16). When we put on masks or work to present a certain perfection, we don't smell so good to the watching world. Our supposed "perfection" doesn't minister to anyone. Instead, it creates distance and slows our clients' growth.

What would be different for your clients if you were not genuine?

Without this quality, coaching would be shallow and transactional. If either person is unwilling to strip off his or her mask, a false posture toward the other is displayed. If it is the coach who is not genuine, the engagement is selfish, because the coach is putting self and image above service to the client. The genuine coach works in service to the client's needs. Without a genuine coach, clients may not connect with the deeper parts of themselves or be able to make the transformational progress they desire.

What would you share with our readers to bring this all together?

A genuine coach creates an invitation for their client to connect deeply with themselves and who they are through the safe and human space of the coaching relationship. When we show up as a genuine coach, we create the environment for our clients to move in a powerful way toward their goals.

What would you say to a coach who wants to grow in being genuine?

Genuineness can only come from the inside. It's hard to feel comfortable with yourself if you don't know yourself. Start with growing in your self-awareness; get to know more of who you are and what matters to you, and then you can begin to connect your true self as a person with you as a coach. Engage with the additional questions below to help develop self-awareness, as it is foundational to becoming genuine and to leading both yourself and others. It is important work that will enable you to live the life God has for you and to be the coach God has created you to be.

For Your Off-Road Journey:

❖ What do you sense gets in the way of your being genuine?

❖ Begin to notice the emotions you are feeling in a given moment and what you do with them.

❖ Experiment with appropriate vulnerability in both non-coaching and coaching conversations.

➤ What happens when you show a bit more of your humanity?

➤ What is appropriate vulnerability to you?

❖ What could happen for your clients if you moved toward being more genuine?

❖ What's one step you would like to experiment with toward dropping your mask and becoming more genuine with yourself, your clients, and others?

IMPARTING
Georgia Shaffer

"For I long to see you, that I may impart to you some spiritual gift to strengthen you—that is, that we may be mutually encouraged by each other's faith, both yours and mine."
Romans 1:11-12 (ESV)

When I first began my coach training, there was so much I did not know about being a professional certified coach. It was especially unsettling to me when I realized that some of my skills as a licensed psychologist in Pennsylvania would actually hinder my ability to partner with my coaching clients.

What Cheryl has imparted to me over the years and continues to share has become the essence of the coach I am today. The following are a few examples of how she generously passed on to me her support and encouragement as well as her coaching knowledge and experience.

Cheryl taught me through example the importance of understanding how intimidating the coaching experience can be for the client. As my mentor coach, Cheryl never demanded perfection. She celebrated every little success.

Recording many of my coaching sessions for her to hear and later discuss was a humbling process for me as a perfectionist. Invariably, as soon as I hit the record button for one of these sessions, I was flooded with anxiety. I could not think clearly nor focus on anything my client was saying.

But Cheryl's encouraging, nonjudgmental manner and acknowledgement of the pressure I felt to do a great job created a safe space. It was a space where I could hear what at times was difficult to hear, but also a space where I could continue to focus on growing as a coach.

A few of the gems she shared that have empowered me as a coach are her emphasis on the power of a pause in a coaching conversation and how the simple phrase "bye for now" could turn a potentially awkward ending of a coaching relationship into an open door for future opportunities to work together.

Her frequent reminder to keep a certain emotional distance from my clients has been invaluable. When I'm carried away by my emotions, I can't see past my own hurts or sense of injustice. It's at those times that my compassion can quickly turn into the need to rescue my client.

Unfortunately, this happened to me when one of my coaching clients started a new job. Before her first day of work, her new manager told the staff what a pro my client was at building productive teams. At that point, the younger women on staff decided they did not like Tiffany (not her real name) before she even began the job.

Tiffany's first day could have been a scene from "Mean Girls." The staff provided her with a laptop with a dead battery and no power cord. Once she found a new battery, she discovered the software she needed for work had never been updated. As she shared with me how they whispered and mocked her, I grew angrier and angrier. Instead of recognizing I was emotionally hooked, I immediately jumped in with suggestions of how she could resolve this issue.

It wasn't until later, when I had time to reflect, that I could see my response was not what was best for my client. As Cheryl says, "You want to connect with your client but not be caught up emotionally."

Most important, Cheryl has taught me to be a coach who transforms lives. In order for that to happen, I need to focus on our Lord and His Holy Spirit power to guide me as He shapes the lives of my clients.

For Your Off-Road Journey:

- ❖ Who has imparted powerful lessons to you along your coaching journey?
- ❖ How have you shown them gratitude for their investment in you?
- ❖ How can you grow as a person that is remembered for the ways you have imparted support, wisdom, knowledge, and experience to others?

End Note:

1. Examples in this chapter have been previously shared in an article for *Christian Coaching Today*, Vol. 1, No. 1, 2023.

INTUITIVE
Marc Ottestad

"So God created man in his own image, in the image of God
he created him; male and female he created them."
Genesis 1:27 (ESV)

The thought of man/woman created with eyes to see, ears
to hear, and hearts to turn toward our Savior Jesus brings to
mind both wonder and gratitude. As coaches we use our eyes
and our ears, then we take these inputs and aim for the heart.
This connects to the concept of intuition, which is connected
deeply with coaching. Humbly and intentionally gathering
information from what we see and hear and sharing it with
permission can give the coach access to a client's heart, and in
turn, inspire the client's growth. As we seek to coach those we

work with, we realize our intuition plays a vital role as we navigate life with our clients.

When I hear the word intuition, I see the face and feel the presence of Cheryl, my coach, mentor, inspiration, and friend. Intuition has a fluidity of care and curiosity that surfaces from spoken and unspoken words. Cheryl uses intuition lightly yet firmly to raise possibilities for her clients. Intuition is the unique tip of a relational spear that pokes and prods into the inner recesses of the soul, allowing the puzzle pieces of life to connect and forming new, treasured pieces for growth. It is often characterized as "reading between the lines" or "reading the tea leaves." It has the sense of knowing what is not known.

When Cheryl uses her intuition, she demonstrates an anticipatory position rather than a position of expectation. This posture is inspirational for me. When I watch Cheryl offer the freedom to "try on" new thinking, it creates wonder and hope. Her example propels me to slow down to be "in the moment *with*"—listening, wondering, and lifting-up intuitive bridges for clients.

Cheryl has elevated my awareness of the powerful use of intuition in coaching. I've witnessed how it creates a warm certainty for clients that we are listening deeply—effectively creating a "listening interpersonal sanctuary"—as we attend to all manner of what is being said and interpret it all with and for our clients. Such a sanctuary builds confidence in clients as they begin to see different possibilities through the words and intonations we share.

Cheryl has also shown me that a significant factor in the successful use of intuition is in how we share our impressions. I have witnessed the way she shares her thoughts with softness and care while also communicating that her idea may be "off track" as she offers her perspective. This commitment to gently and humbly share an insight helps build a special relationship with clients that can play a huge, affirming role with those we serve while also opening the way to connect deeply with them.

As a coach, I want such connections. I want to allow my intuition to take form. I want to be courageous to share with my clients the possibilities so that they may see something new. I want to hold the intuitive ideas lightly and allow them to either land or float away. I want to remember that intuition is a key tool in one's toolbelt that can bring new horizons, new hope, comfort, and care to the coaching process.

When a client experiences the gift of intuition, it is bonding. As the recipient of Cheryl's intuition, I have felt seen and been helped to see myself. My desire to trust someone with me is fulfilled by the trustworthiness Cheryl has demonstrated. When Cheryl sits in the coach's seat there is an expectation that she will see, intuit, and reveal, thus creating something new from her skill and love.

Yes, Cheryl's use of intuition feels like love.

When Cheryl models intuition, I am changed as a man and a coach. As I have witnessed her practice of intuition, I have come to believe that intuition is a muscle that grows with exercise. Central to this belief is the understanding that using intuition and exploration is neither right nor wrong; instead, it is a relationship-building process that comes to life through context and possibility.

What makes being intuitive essential for a coach is the process of revelation. We help clients break free from limiting beliefs and draw out areas where they need growth. Intuition plays a role in both instances as a thread into the inner recesses of a client. Intuition is part of a slow-motion replay with a new filter for viewing. As a coach, I hope to move toward deeper listening and relationships. Intuition opens that possibility. It is the doorway into the unknown as it connects the spoken and unspoken.

Using intuition often feels a little scary. There are whispers of "wrong direction," "this might be harmful," or "I am off base." There is a counterweight to these thoughts centered on humility and love. These are attributes of Jesus, and the Holy Spirit always helps by pointing us back to Jesus. The possibilities, the newness, and the release of distorted thinking result in hope. Yes, there may be whispers of doubt, but God is greater, and hope is fuel for growth.

Cheryl has paved the path forward for us off-roaders to learn to live out the use of intuition as a gift from God to love other people.

We all serve in a broken world, a world of rupture and repair. It started in the Garden, where God declared:

"So God created man in his own image, in the image of God he created him; male and female he created them" (Genesis 1:27, ESV).

God's own image is perfect wholeness. Yes, we are broken, and yes, God provides a way back. As we learn to use intuition in our coaching, it opens the way for God to bring forth mighty works of repair. In so doing, intuition becomes a God-given gift toward redemption.

For Your Off-Road Journey:

* *Explore helping your clients tap into their own intuition and trust their inner voice.*

* *Explore your leaning toward logic and reason as a coach, as well as the possibility that you are moving away from intuition.*

❖ *How to grow intuition:*

> ➤ *Mindfulness, by quieting yourself through meditation and deep breathing.*

> ➤ *Pay attention to hunches and feelings—your inner voice.*

> ➤ *Develop your intuition muscle. Start small, listen, and act.*

> ➤ *Expand your senses. Pay attention to your God-given senses.*

> ➤ *Seek feedback. Explore your intuitions with others.*

RESILIENT
Jennifer Grote

"But the seed in the good ground—these are the ones who, having heard the word with an honest and good heart, hold on to it and by enduring, produce fruit."
Luke 8:15 (CSB)

Resilience is the capacity to withstand or recover quickly from difficulties, a trait many of us would welcome in increasing measure. However, we often underestimate our own resilience until we're faced with unexpected and difficult circumstances.

Halfway through 2020, the world was scrambling to adjust to a worldwide pandemic. In addition to stressors "out there," I was reeling from inner stressors, things bombarding my head and heart. On a sunny morning in June, feeling wound up and anxious, I sought stretching to alleviate my stress. Without warming up or thinking too much, I swiftly assumed an advanced yoga pose. Coming out of the pose and sitting up straight, the room spun. My lips and face started to tingle and feel numb while my vision became blurry. I scrambled around the floor, trying to locate my phone. Unable to see clearly, I called my husband but got his voicemail. As tingling and numbness ensued, a wave of panic swept over me, and I dialed 911. After an MRI and several hours of waiting in the emergency room, they sent me home. Despite feeling as though something was terribly wrong, every test came back as normal. To the medical world I appeared fine, but I knew I was not.

My life became marred by migraines, double vision, panic attacks, and problems balancing. Despite seeing an array of specialists, explanations eluded them. With my body on the fritz, my mind continually wondered, "What's wrong with me?"

Eighteen months passed. At the urging of my psychiatrist, who advocated for a new MRI, the truth came to light. A very important artery had torn in my neck, causing much mayhem, including two strokes in my right and left cerebellum. Something had been terribly wrong, and I sensed it, but listening to doctors over my intuition for such an extended time had left me feeling crazy. Very crazy.

Having answers paved the way to true healing, both mentally and spiritually. One of the first things my psychiatrist instructed me to do was to "assemble my team." My team was Jesus, my husband, a new neurologist, and Dr. Ose, Director of Holistic Mental Health, PLLC. Physically, the damage was done; we would have to wait and see if my body would heal or whether surgery would be warranted. They checked my progress through regular scans. I also began an intense process of emotional healing through EMDR (eye movement desensitization and reprocessing therapy).

Less than a year following my diagnosis, my final scan indicated my body was healing enough that I wouldn't need surgery. The pathway of healing was in its final stretch as the hardest days were now behind me.

Through all of this, I developed a deep, sweet intimacy with the Lord. In my state of vulnerability, I was available to Him and to the work He wanted to do in my heart. My roots descended, unfurling deep into the soil and anchoring my faith in place. There were buckets of ungrieved grief. I mourned over sins, regrets, mistakes, and losses. I was unraveling and unabashedly letting go, releasing a lifetime of what I'd been holding on to and what Jesus was asking me to give to Him.

Could I have grown to the depths I have grown had my situation not unfolded the terrible way it did? There's no way to know; but I do know I'm a different person now—a more resilient one. When we cling to Christ, facing uncertainty means that good things can come out of bad situations. And for that, I am eternally grateful. Luke 8:15 tells us that by enduring we produce fruit. Enduring means to suffer patiently; to remain in existence; to last. A similar word is to abide.

In John 15:4, Jesus says, "Abide in me, and I in you. As the branch cannot bear fruit by itself, unless it abides in the vine, neither can you, unless you abide in me" (ESV). What is this fruit? The Bible tells us in Galatians 5: 22-23: "But the fruit of the Spirit is love, joy, peace, patience, kindness, goodness, faithfulness, gentleness, and self-control" (ESV).

Resilience isn't a trait we all naturally embody. As Christians, when we choose to continually abide and bear fruit, we are becoming ever more resilient. Why is this important to a Christian coach? As a coach, we often stand in the gap for our clients. We stand in the gap between the "already" (where they are now) and the "not yet" (where they want to go). We nurture the spaces between a seed being planted and its taking root, and between the roots growing deep and the branches bearing fruit.

Cheryl has stood in that gap for me. Through her ministry, Promised Land Living, she helped me see the gap between my sense of identity in the world and my identity in Christ. Seeds were planted in my heart through this ministry. Many I was unaware of, but they bore fruit—especially during my two years of hardship.

Cheryl also stood in the gap as my personal coach. She introduced me to the idea that I needed to allow the Lord to develop my capacity to endure (Holy Spirit-led foreshadowing, perhaps?). The gaps were in my thinking, between how I thought things should be and how they really were, as well as in my own spiritual maturity. In fact, I can remember a quote she shared that I used as wallpaper on my iPhone for many, many months: "No grit, no pearl!"

Cheryl has stood in the gap as my mentor through Coach's Edge. She has modeled and demonstrated the skills, knowledge, and characteristics of an off-roader, especially resilience. Cheryl has suffered and endured Stage 4 neurological Lyme disease. She would often share stories of how sick she was and how dire her situation was. Seeing her in front of us, leading several successful businesses and a ministry, was a beacon of hope. If she could endure, maybe I could too!

One evening, Cheryl showed up to our Coach's Edge meeting in what looked like some kind of torture device. She was in a back brace that limited her ability to move, to include even moving her head from side to side. She had fallen off a horse and broken her back, but she was fully present for us even though it meant showing up injured and limited.

What did that do for me? It showed a level of authenticity, transparency, and determination, as well as a belief in something greater than herself. I wanted that for myself— permission to show up even when showing up was hard and awkward. Her resolve demonstrated the capacity to withstand the trials of life with an honest and good heart, a sense of humor, and the capacity to not only recover but also to endure and bear fruit. In today's world, most everything is photoshopped. It's easy to think that success means looking and being perfect all the time. Cheryl offers a different, truer picture of success.

It's been said that a coach can only take a client as far as they've been willing to go. Our clients are looking for proof. Proof that they can, or that they can't. They're straddling the fence of "already" and "not yet." They're questioning whether the journey is worth it.

As you develop your own resiliency, you stand in the gap for your clients as they develop their own. Your awareness of your own resiliency will enable you to believe it for them while they build their own ability to endure and bear fruit.

For Your Off-Road Journey:

- ❖ What trials have you endured, and how might you leverage those in your coaching?
- ❖ How might you reframe a current challenge through the lens of resilience?
- ❖ What comes up for you as you read this quote aloud?

"It is not the critic who counts; not the man who points out how the strong man stumbles, or where the doer of deeds could have done them

better. The credit belongs to the man who is actually in the arena, whose face is marred by dust and sweat and blood; who strives valiantly; who errs, who comes short again and again, because there is no effort without error and shortcoming; but who does actually strive to do the deeds; who knows great enthusiasms, the great devotions; who spends himself in a worthy cause; who at the best knows in the end the triumph of high achievement, and who at the worst, if he fails, at least fails while daring greatly."
—*Theodore Roosevelt*

TRANSFORMATIVE
A Conversation with Jim Woodward

*"Do not conform to the pattern of this world, but be
transformed by the renewing of your mind. Then you will
be able to test and approve what God's will is—his good,
pleasing and perfect will."*
Romans 12:2 (NIV)

Clients do not hire coaches merely as a financial
transaction—they want to experience some form of change.
Jim Woodward and I discussed a character quality that sets the
conditions for these changes. Let's explore what it means to be
transformative and notice the beauty God creates through a
coach who exhibits this quality.

How would you describe the quality of being transformative?

Most people have experienced an "aha" moment, like a light bulb going on. Being transformative is helping someone see things in a new way. Illumination has a cascading effect; from that point, a person starts to put the pieces of their story together differently. When someone has new light, they start to see how they can reorder the way they have been approaching important parts of their life.

What about being transformative inspires you?

It's a joy to see a possibility that I've not seen before. When I left the company that I helped start, my pastor asked me, "What does this make possible?" That powerful question energized me to look down the path God called me to, which is helping people achieve their potential and grow closer to Jesus.

What makes being transformative essential for a coach?

It's essential for a coach to be transformative because coaches are trying to help people get unstuck. We start by holding up a mirror to help clients see themselves and their situations differently—to notice what they haven't seen before. Clients can't climb a hill if they don't know it's there!

What do you notice in yourself as you experience your coach being transformative?

One of my Clifton strengths is "achiever"—I'm oriented to get things done. But I used to regularly accuse myself of being a procrastinator when I wasn't working on something. Cheryl helped me see my nonworking periods as times to grow and get reenergized for what was important to me. Because Cheryl is a transformative coach, she helped me see patterns in my marriage differently; that helped my wife and I change the narrative of our marriage. Bottom line: When my coach is transformative, I see things differently and get unstuck, and that changes my lifelong patterns.

Your coach being transformative illuminated something for you that changed your patterns and your path.
Yes! Whenever Cheryl noticed me slipping into an old pattern, she'd say, "Jim, you're doing that to yourself again." She was "in my corner," and I even sensed her pain as she noticed what I was doing to myself. That pattern didn't break loose all at once; just like Jesus with His disciples, it took time and repetition.

Jesus was <u>with</u> the disciples; Cheryl was <u>with</u> you. So there's a <u>with-ness</u> to being transformative.
Cheryl's with-ness conveyed a shared desire for breakthrough. She wanted it for me as much as I did—maybe even more than I did at the beginning! What an incredible partnership to have someone be transformative with me and for me, and to see the impact of that part of her character on all aspects of my life, including my coaching.

What does being transformative as a coach make possible for your clients?
Being transformative helps me hear things in different ways— if I notice a client's tone is different than normal, that opens the door to explore what's going on with him or her below the surface. I learned that from Cheryl too—she'd "call out" when I came to a session with a different presence! Doing this helped

me to have a very different and more powerful conversation than I had planned.

"Calling out what you notice" jumpstarts your clients' transformation. What else does being transformative bring to clients?

Most of my leadership clients want to focus on practical *doing* topics—getting their business from point A to point B. Because I prioritize transformation, I also engage in their *being* by saying and asking things that help them get from A to B faster than they could by focusing on *doing* alone.

What beauty is God creating in your clients because you are transformative?

The CEOs and other business leaders I'm coaching can easily get stuck working *in the business* instead of *on the business*. That often results in them focusing on the whirlwind of the day but not making time for their most important relationships. When I shed light on this, God creates beauty as they begin to experience more joy and blessing in their lives. After Cheryl shined the light on an important principle by sharing the famous "Who's Got the Monkey?" article[1] with me, God helped me create beauty as leaders I coached moved from drudgery and burden to lightness by empowering their people. And their families were impacted too!

What other beauty is God creating in your coaching because you are transformative?

God is also creating beauty in the lives of my clients as they grasp the importance of refueling and reconnecting with God and their families. God rested and calls us to rest, but many CEOs ignore that. So I shine the light on what Scripture says and then help them see ways to make time for refueling. It's beautiful to see leaders working on what's most important and having the energy to make a real difference as the Holy Spirit brings them transformation. And there's beauty in all the ripple effects.

What final word would you like to share with our readers?
To be transformative for someone, you must love them with *agape* love—the love that seeks what's best for them regardless of the cost to you. That might involve pointing out how they're stuck, which can be risky if that's something they don't want to see! So your coaching partnership might be negatively impacted. But if you love them, you don't hold back; you're bold enough to step into the opportunity and self-sacrifice to be with them and for them.

For Your Off-Road Journey:
❖ *What makes being more transformative important to you?*
❖ *What "telltales" help you watch for transformative opportunities?*
❖ *What will help you draw out the "why" behind your client's "what"?*

End Note:
1. Oncken Jr., William, and Wass, Donald L. "Management Time: Who's Got the Monkey?" *Harvard Business Review*, November-December 1974.

OUR INVITATION

"Two people are better off than one, for they can help each other succeed."
Ecclesiastes 4:9 (NLT)

We pray that you have grown in your appreciation for many of the character qualities of an off-roading coach and that you have also begun the process of further developing one or more of these qualities. We all grew in our own understanding of these qualities by co-creating this book, and God graciously created "over and above" beauty by deepening our relationships with one another in the process. We now invite you to expand both your learning and your relational joy by connecting with other coaches to explore character qualities we have not investigated here.

A Sampling of Off-Roader Coach Qualities We Have Not Explored in the Book:

❖ **Humble:** An off-roader knows and admits they haven't "arrived"; they are open to growth and comfortable "not knowing."

❖ **Curious:** An off-roader consistently demonstrates deep interest in every aspect of what the client is sharing, for the client's sake.

❖ **Inspiring:** An off-roader calls their client up to the next level of development.

❖ **Generous:** An off-roader graciously shares their life and their story.

❖ **Sense of Humor:** An off-roader laughs (often at themselves), putting a client at ease.

A Fun Way to Explore These Qualities

Invite at least one other coach to have a conversation with you about one of the qualities listed above (or another quality that comes to mind). Using the guidelines below, interview each other about this quality.

Rapport-building and relational warm-up

❖ Come to your conversation with deep appreciation for your fellow coach(es) and their desire to encourage and sharpen each other.

❖ Consider opening your conversation with prayer and enjoying some small talk.

❖ Thank your fellow coach(es) for their willingness to have a conversation with you about this quality and its importance to a coach and their clients.

❖ Ask each other 2-3 questions from each of the sections below.

The meaning of this quality

❖ What scripture or quote captures the essence of this quality for you?

❖ What does this quality mean to you?

❖ What about this quality inspires (or is "life-giving for" or "energizing for") you?

❖ Who best demonstrates this quality for you?

❖ What does this quality look and/or feel like? What story or stories come to mind when you think about this quality?

The implications of and/or importance of this quality to you as a coach

❖ What makes this quality essential for a coach?

❖ What is different about you because someone has modeled it for you?

❖ What do you notice (see, feel, etc.) as you experience this quality in or receive this quality from someone?

❖ How is this quality impacting you as a coach?

❖ What does this quality bring to other aspects of your life?

The implications of and/or impact of this quality on your coaching and your clients

❖ What difference does this quality make in (or what does this quality bring to) your coaching?

❖ What does this quality open up (or "make possible") for your clients?

❖ What beauty (or "life," etc. … pick the word that resonates most for you) does God create in your coaching thru this quality?

❖ What would be different for your clients if you didn't have this quality?

❖ What else does this quality bring to your clients?

Growing in this quality

❖ What would be different if you had 10% more of this quality?

❖ What tiny habit will catalyze your growth in this quality?

❖ What question would you ask another coach who wants to grow in this quality?

Life-giving ways to consolidate your learning

After your interview, we invite you to take one or more of these actions:

❖ Co-author an article or blog post based on your conversation.

❖ Write a journal entry about your conversation.

❖ Write an affirmation about a coach who has positively impacted your life by demonstrating this character quality, then deliver the affirmation to this coach.

AFTERWORD: "ROOTED"
Todd Kemp

In a conversation with Scott Frickenstein and fellow contributors after we had completed the initial editing of our chapters, I had an "Aha!" moment that sparked this opportunity to invite our readers to a peek behind the curtain of this volume, its contributors, and our beloved mentor-coach-teacher, Cheryl Scanlan.

The reality is that each of us is in process. Like pine trees that grow from pinecones in loamy soil and reach skyward as they sway in the breeze, these coaches have grown in their character through a growth process that requires being rooted. As pines need to be rooted in nutrient-rich soil with adequate moisture, we need to be rooted in a source of character-forming "nutrients" to grow as healthy, vibrant, and "fruitful" people.

The growth process, however, cannot be willed. As capable and accomplished as one may be, a person is unable to find the nutrients within themselves to grow their own character. We need others to give us nutrients to help us grow in the most important ways—relationally, emotionally, and spiritually. Notably, coaching can be an important and productive way to help people in their growth journey.

Wherever you are on your own path of exploring, discovery, and becoming, we welcome and honor you. Admittedly, this is an odd thing to say at the end of a book. But what became evident to me as I dialogued with my collaborators is that readers might be coming from very different backgrounds, and someone who reads this might benefit from having more context around this labor of love for Cheryl and for you, our reader. I hope that this peek behind the curtain will shed valuable light on the basis for the formation and growth of these character traits in each of us.

Throughout these pages, you've seen references to Bible passages, God, Jesus, the Holy Spirit, and other signposts that mark a contributor's spiritual perspective and how that viewpoint informs their outlook on a given character quality. If you have a new, distant, or even no relationship with such matters, the following paragraphs are written especially for you.

First, you have my genuine respect for reading this far and holding a curiosity that likely serves you and others well. Second, I want to set your mind at ease and let you know that my intention isn't to fix you or anyone else or to convince you of anything. Rather, I aim to share more about the spiritual dimension these co-laborers have in common and how it gives life to their coaching, and invite you to continue to explore, at your own pace, the significance it might hold for you.

To begin this further exploration, I'd like to offer a question for your consideration. When have you felt fully known and truly loved *for who you are*, and what was that like for you? Before you read further, I invite you to pause and ponder this question.

According to the Bible, each of us was created in the image of God and given authority to create order in the world for the benefit of others. It says God loves us and desires to have a relationship with us and, importantly, He gives us freedom in the development of that relationship.

Each of us in our own ways have turned away from or ignored God, whether actively fighting against or simply excluding God from our lives. Instead of using our authority for good, we sometimes hurt others, do things for selfish gain, or turn a blind eye to injustice. The Bible calls this sin, whether it's our attitude or action. As God's image-bearers, we all fall short of the glory and splendor of His character. The consequences, according to the Bible, are sobering. Just as we work to earn a paycheck, the wages due to us for our sin is death—both physical and spiritual—which includes separation from God.

But God, in His loving-kindness toward us, gave us the only perfect gift to restore the broken relationship between He and us so that we may experience true, abundant life now and forever. He gave us the gift of Jesus, His Son, who bore the wages of our sin. Though He was sinless, He died a criminal's death, was buried, and, by the power of God, was resurrected after three days according to many eyewitnesses and as was foretold by the ancient Hebrew Scriptures.

The gift is free to us, though it cost God enormously. Yet, as with all gifts given to us, our part is to receive the gift of Jesus. To accept this gift, Jesus invites us to put our faith in Him as the one who reconciles us to God. As St. Paul writes, "If you openly declare that Jesus is Lord and believe in your heart that God raised him from the dead, you will be saved" (NLT). To declare that "Jesus is Lord" is to yield leadership of our life to Him.

For me personally, this life with Jesus has meant experiencing joy amid the sorrows, hope during dark days, and purpose despite the pain, as well as letting go of things I can't control while trusting that God is for me and that He is leading me in a better way. As I receive God's love for me, I know it to be genuine and powerful since He knows me fully and truly loves me *for who I am*. This love overflows and gives my life and coaching a different aroma than it otherwise would have.

For each of these coach-contributors and for our friend Cheryl, Jesus is the foundation of all the character qualities that we've shared with you and more. Without Jesus guiding our lives, we're not able to show up this way consistently, holistically, or to significant degrees for our clients or anyone else. As we trust God more fully with who we are and join Him in the work He is doing in our hearts and minds, He grows our character over time. As one of our contributors has said, Jesus is the Master Coach. As we allow ourselves to be coached and led by Jesus, He is present to us in ways that we most need, to help us see, learn, grow, love others, and receive love beyond our innate capacities. As I've said, we are still in process; none of us has arrived. Jesus doesn't force Himself on anyone, yet He is our most powerful ally and dearest friend.

As contributors of this book who are in the process of transformation through Jesus, we invite you to continue to pursue and respond to the truth of Jesus in your own way. As St. Paul, who had a dramatic story of coming to faith in Jesus, writes:

"I pray that out of [God's] glorious riches he may strengthen you with power through his Spirit in your inner being, so that [Jesus] Christ may dwell in your hearts through faith. And I pray that you, being rooted and established in love, may have power, together with all the Lord's holy people, to grasp how wide and long and high and deep is the love of [Jesus] Christ, and to know this love that surpasses knowledge— that you may be filled to the measure of all the fullness of God."
Ephesians 3:16-19 (NIV)

May you continue to explore, discover, and become rooted in this great love of Jesus!

— Todd Kemp, MCC, May 2023, Larkspur, Colorado

Additional Resources for Discovery:

"Character of God" video series – 6 videos about God's character by The Bible Project:

https://bibleproject.com/explore/category/character-of-god-series/

Gospel of John from the Bible—read about Jesus from an eyewitness account:

https://www.biblestudytools.com/john/

"Gospel of the Kingdom" – video explanation of the Gospel (5:48) by The Bible Project:

https://bibleproject.com/explore/video/gospel-kingdom/

Groundwire—virtual chat with a live spiritual coach about your questions of faith:

https://www.groundwire.net/chat

The Chosen TV series—multi-season streaming TV series about the life and ministry of Jesus of Nazareth and his early followers:

https://thechosen.tv/

ACKNOWLEDGMENTS

We are all eternally grateful to God for graciously creating beauty through a process that has challenged us, encouraged us, and forged us into friends. We are humbled that Jesus called us to Himself and called us to be coaches. We are thankful for Cheryl Scanlan's deep investment in our coaching competence *and* our character. The ripple effect she has had in the lives of our clients and in our character may not be fully known on this side of heaven, but we've felt it and we want to honor it.

We're also grateful to our clients, who give us the opportunity to live out our competence and grow in our character, and to our entire Coach's Edge community for sharpening us through our life-giving engagements. We could not have completed this task without the clandestine cooperation of Brittany Thieman, our outstanding community manager, who advised me on presenting our work to Cheryl as a surprise.

I want to personally acknowledge my bride for selflessly transcribing and editing several hours of interviews; my coaches Ty Saltzgiver, Bruce McNicol, and Eric Ludwig for partnering with me as I discerned God's leading in the conceptual stages of this effort; and my longtime friend Edie Edmondson for her incredible gift of professionally editing our entire manuscript.

I'm also profoundly grateful to Mark Ross for graciously commissioning a new work of art for this effort, to Chad Bartlett for designing a beautiful cover, to Kathleen Fischer for her heartfelt and tireless partnership in the final phases, to Michele Chynoweth for preparing our manuscript for publishing, and to each contributor for selflessly journeying with me to create something truly beautiful. To God be the glory!

—Scott Frickenstein

CONTRIBUTORS

Kathleen Fischer, CPLC

Kathleen is the founder of Christ-Centered Success and the Christ-Empowered Entrepreneurs' Journey. She is a professional coach and speaker who equips passionate women of God to walk in the power of Christ as they fulfill God's call to build successful businesses and joy-filled lives.

Kathleen brings a holistic approach to her work, equipping women to overcome both the internal and external challenges that are hindering their success. She also combines her coach training with her background as a systems analyst to equip her clients to experience success in both Christ-centeredness and business-building solutions.

On the personal side, Kathleen is a lover of everything created by God—people, nature, and the wonder of life. She lives in historic Rhode Island with her husband of more than 38 years, who shares her love for their two adult children and families. You'll most often find Kathleen outdoors, hiking, gardening, paddle-boarding, cycling, and playing in the ocean waves.

Kathleen's dream is to see a multitude of women worldwide who are fully alive in Christ, joyfully and powerfully fulfilling the amazing works God has created them to do!

Scott Frickenstein, PhD, PCC

Scott was raised in Wisconsin and grew up loving to learn and lead. He was selected to attend the U.S. Air Force Academy and served as an Air Force officer for more than 25 years. Scott held multiple C-level, higher education, and analytical roles and retired as a colonel after leading thousands of airmen and publishing articles in several disciplines. One of Scott's call signs was "Coach" because of his heart for helping people discover and reach their personal and professional potential.

Scott was deeply impacted by many coaches, mentors, and teachers, so he's devoted his "second half" to developing leaders, utilizing his learner's mindset and pastor's heart. He launched Leading by Design to invest in faith-based nonprofit leaders, and he coaches business leaders through WeAlign Coaching. Scott enjoys coaching individuals, couples, and teams; speaking frequently on leader development; and teaching and mentoring newer coaches.

Wende Gaikema, MBA, PCC

Wende is an executive and leadership coach who helps leaders develop their business and their people. Wende works with executives, leaders, and teams to build their skills in leadership presence, EQ, influential communication, change management, and personal and team effectiveness.

Wende's leadership experience includes extensive and increasingly responsible roles at Procter & Gamble in brand management, sales, and operations. She has served on multiple boards and chaired the board of directors for a large nonprofit.

Wende and her husband, Jeff, have been married for 31 years and have three sons—one in heaven and two on earth. She enjoys outdoor recreation and ministering to people with her certified therapy dogs.

Jennifer Grote, Certified HWC, Strengths Champion Certified Coach

Jennifer had the makings of a life coach from a young age. She was often interested in the inner thoughts and feelings of others. Her family would chuckle when little "Jenny" (age 5 or 6) would ask adults to sit down and tell her about their day. Attuned, she would empathize and ask still more questions.

Professionally, Jennifer has held multiple roles in sales and leadership across industries. Before leaving to start her coaching business, she was an area director of sales for a large home health and hospice organization. It was during that time that Jennifer began to feel restless. Perhaps it was working with people who were near the end of their lives, but she began to think about her path, her passion, and her purpose. She invited two of her closest friends to meet with her once a month to discuss their hopes, dreams, and goals. Each person's life was completely transformed. Jennifer knew she wanted more of whatever "this" was. She then discovered life coaching and went on to become a Certified Life & Wellbeing Coach through Duke Health & Wellbeing, and a Strengths Champion Certified Coach. Now, Jennifer works with high-achieving women who have that restless feeling inside of them and may be wondering about their own path, passion, and purpose. She helps them get unstuck and then move forward with clarity, confidence, and courage.

Todd Kemp, MA, MCC

"Where do you want to go?" is a question that has resonated with Todd since high school, when a mentor asked about his life ambitions. It propelled him to new adventures beyond the small Central California farm where he grew up, including being part of two NCAA championship teams, playing for the U.S. National Water Polo Team, running IT projects on three continents, and leading sales/systems engineering teams at a Fortune 150 tech firm. Todd also pursued three entrepreneurial ventures, including one debacle, which earned him a lot of scar tissue and fostered great respect for business owners and leaders who care about their people and want to grow as leaders.

Coaching with curiosity, compassion, and courage, Todd helps these leaders and their teams explore their own adventures in pursuing inside-out growth and building transformative cultures to create more value, experience greater well-being, and integrate a greater purpose. He and his bride, Julianne, have two young-adult children and live in Colorado, where they enjoy outdoor adventuring together.

Kiley Lee, ACC, LCSW

Kiley is an executive and life coach who has been helping people change for more than 20 years, beginning her lifelong career of helping people as a clinical social worker in transitional housing, university, and outpatient mental health settings.

As a coach, Kiley particularly enjoys working with women leaders and nonprofit executive directors who want to develop their own strengths, self-awareness, leadership abilities, and teams in order to impact the world for good.

Kiley is known for her relational style, sense of humor, directness, and fierce commitment to unleashing the very best in her clients.

Kiley lives in San Diego with her husband and two kids, coaching at a standing desk while her dog, Sadie, snoozes next to her in the recliner. She enjoys reading fiction, being outdoors, eating chocolate, and being beaten by her 12-year-old at Wordle nearly every day. She'd love for you to start a conversation with her on LinkedIn.

Pamela Mertz, PCC

Pamela is the president and founder of BluePrint Life Coaching LLC, a leadership life coach, a speaker, and an author.

She transitioned from 35+ years as a business founder/owner in a high-tech industry to coaching in 2017. Her experience also includes positions on for-profit and nonprofit boards of directors, leading and guiding organizations through transition and acquisition. Pamela brings more than 20 years' experience in ministry leadership positions as well.

She is a certified leadership life coach and is on faculty at PCCI. She is a certified Quality Improvement Coach for healthcare teams by IEHSS at the University of New Hampshire, a certified Strengths Finders Coach, and a certified facilitator for Partnership Enhancement through Academy of Communication in Healthcare (ACH) for the Cystic Fibrosis Foundation. One of her favorite roles is as director of coach presenters at Promised Land Living, a nonprofit, international ministry of discipleship in how to live and remain in that promised, abundant life in Christ.

As a mentor-coach, Pamela enjoys supporting other coaches to achieve their credentialing objectives and fortify their coaching skills.

She is a newly published author of the first in a God-help series titled "Truth About Church Wounds." This book is an interactive group Bible study on healing and restoration for the Church. She is working on her second "God-help" series book titled "Listen *IN*."

Pamela is married to Lou and is mother to three adult sons and a beautiful daughter in love. She lives in Minnesota and enjoys gardening, biking, hiking, and a newfound love of pickleball!

Marc Ottestad

Marc is president and founder of Legacy Coaching LLC and the Southern California director for CBMC. Over the past 50 years Marc has led organizations in hospitality, retail, and leadership development. In Marc's hospitality season, he opened and operated a dozen restaurants and entertainment facilities. This work had the greatest impact on his life as he connected with his wife of 43 years, Kasey, creating the foundation of a good life that includes three children—Toby, Kristin, and David—as well as grandchildren.

With Kasey's encouragement, Marc created a pathway out of hospitality by completing his degree in finance at Cal State Fullerton in 1985. His degree opened the door that resulted in his retail season. Over the next 20 years, as a partner at Pro Sound and Stage Lighting (PSSL), Marc recruited, developed, and strategically grew the enterprise to 125 employees and gained a position as a national leader in the sound and lighting industry. It was in this season of personal and professional challenges that Marc met Jesus.

As the president of PSSL, Marc connected with BBL Forum, a faith-centered peer and coaching leadership development resource. Being encouraged toward centering Jesus, Marc was invited to join BBL Forum, which evolved into Convene. Marc led the recruitment and training of group leaders and membership as God moved. A significant resource for growing the impact of Convene was connecting to PCCI and Cheryl Scanlan, which led to Marc's move into coaching and personal growth, including the privilege of serving as a coach presenter and board member for Promised Land Living.

Mark Ross, MBA, ACC

After a 30-year career in leadership and public service, Mark longed to start a new chapter. He ultimately worked with a coach to help determine his "next thing." Now he helps others discover their next thing as they move into a new season as Encore-preneurs, enjoying the freedom to pursue the life, work, and relationships that matter most. In addition to private clients who are navigating transitions, Mark also serves as a team host with the Rock Retirement Club and as a strategic coach with the REALIFE Process.

Mark lives in Texas with his wife and is the proud father of two grown daughters. One of his deepest joys is creating visual music to inspire the world through expressionistic landscape paintings, and it's an important part of his next thing in this season as an Encore-preneur.

Georgia Shaffer, MA, PCC, MCLC

Georgia equips Christian women through online coaching groups such as ReBUILD After Divorce, Taking Out Your Emotional Trash, Healthy Healing Relationships, and Dating After Divorce. She started the monthly membership ReBUILD group to provide separated and divorced women with a place to learn and the space to grow in a community of Christian women also struggling to begin anew.

She is the author of six books, including "Coaching the Coach," "Taking Out Your Emotional Trash," and "A Gift of Mourning Glories: Restoring Your Life After Loss." Georgia is a recipient of the American Association of Christian

Counselors award for excellence in Christian caregiving.

Her passion is gardening. After the loss of her health, job, and marriage, she found healing and restoration in God's creation. You can find pictures of her garden and free resources at www.GeorgiaShaffer.com.

Cindy Schmelzenbach, MA, PCC

Cindy and Harmon, her husband of more than four decades, believe in fully engaging life wherever God invites them, every moment, every day. They've spent 22 years in entrepreneurial businesses and another 19 years internationally in cross-cultural leadership roles within a global ministry organization. Their passion for holistic health and enhanced team dynamics moved Cindy to develop a member care initiative that she then successfully launched and coordinated across 46 countries in the Asia Pacific region.

Cindy calls herself a conversation coach. Believing deeply that our "words create worlds," she coaches individuals, groups, and teams to explore and become mindful and intentional about the conversations that happen within them, among them, and beyond them. She also provides ICF mentor coaching for individuals and in group contexts.

She and her husband love their kids and grandkids fiercely and are grateful to share life with them in the mountains of southern New Mexico.

Doreen Steenland, PCC, RN

Doreen Steenland is a registered nurse and International Coaching Federation-certified coach and mental fitness expert. Doreen's diverse nursing experience and neuroscience training provide a unique approach to her coaching. She is the founder of Living Full Life Coaching and empowers exhausted medical professionals to rise above their stress patterns, get anchored, and take control again.

Doreen also coaches women who have conquered survival mode and are now ready to live again! Empowering women to disrupt autopilot living to be present and walk in freedom is her passion.

She is a speaker and author of "Transform Your Brain, One Thought At A Time," coming out in 2023.

She lives by grace through faith in New Jersey with her hubby of 32 years and has three adult children. She loves golfing, hiking, and all things outdoors. Her favorite place to rest is her front porch.

Jim Woodward, PCC

Jim is a peer advisory board chair and an ACC-certified business growth coach for Convene in Dallas, Texas. Jim's passion is to help leaders grow high-performing businesses on a biblical foundation so that people thrive and the Kingdom grows.

After building and running businesses as large as $100 million, Jim feels called to help people get unstuck, achieve their potential, and grow closer to Jesus. This is accomplished through peer-to-peer counsel, life-on-life community, and one-on-one coaching. Jim is the author of "The Work Exchange," a six-part video series on what God says about work (www.theworkexchange.org) that has been published by Convene and the Talbot Center for Faith, Work, and Economics. Jim has also designed a variety of other adult learning experiences, including *Answering the Big Questions of Faith, Bible Reading and Reflection, Restoring Freedom to Overloaded Lives, Spiritual Conversations, Teaching to Transform Lives,* and

Transformational Bible Study. Jim is married to Julie, and they have three grown kids.

More About Coach's Edge

You don't have to be lonely as a coach. Coach's Edge offers a place for you to grow your skills as a coach and develop your business, all within the context of a supportive community. After reading this book, if you are interested in learning more about our membership community, we would love to connect with you.

Visit our website to learn more:
https://mentorcoachinsights.com/coachs-edge/

You can also reach out directly to our Community Manager, Brittany, to learn more and ask further questions: brittany@mentorcoachinsights.com

Made in the USA
Monee, IL
28 June 2023